SIREN SONG

Siren Song

Tawni Waters

PUBLISHED BY

BURLESQUE PRESS

Table of Contents

Part Three: From Isis to Osiris

PART ONE

MARY MAGDALENE'S PRAYERS

In Memoriam: from Magdalene to the Crucified Christ

Did I lose the real story when I came to this place?

In visions, I've seen
the darkness that was over the face of the deep
before the

"let there be"

brought this dead world back to life.
Black nothing still hovers here
smothering the memory
of every soul that enters the atmosphere.
We forget the celestial spheres.

My curse is I still half-remember.

When I saw you, I knew
who you were
even though you did not.
It was that knowing that drove me
to give up everything
to be yours.
Pharisees called me crazy,
and I'd think so too
had you not whispered secrets
only God could know,
had not invisible angels
visibly conspired with me
every step of the way.

Darling, I watched you cure lepers.
Darling, we raised the dead.

I read the book. I understood
you would have to die,
though no one told me
I would be crucified too.
When I was taken to the wilderness
to face Satan first
I was stunned.
Until I was staring into the devil's eyes,
I believed I was nothing more
than a whore kissing your feet.
I did not know that there was such
a thing as the

Daughter of God.

I saw the icons. I thought
when you breathed your last,
I'd be kneeling at your cross,
weeping.
I did not know
having conquered death
I would be watching
from some distant paradise,
barely able to see your wounds
that would someday become
sacred scars.

Savior,
this heaven is hell without you.
Divine light lived in your eyes,
but here, surrounded by the holy,
I know
it was your humanity I loved most.
The blood that poured from your mouth
when they broke you

must have tasted like salt.

My king, know this as you weep alone in your tomb.
If I could, I would wash your feet forever.
I would hold your human head against my chest
and make you remember holy.

My love, do not listen to the demons.
Death is an illusion.
When you see that
and fly free

my king
my love
Son of God
Son of Man

fly to me

My sacred lips will kiss you
until you forget the fire.

Descent, An Autumn Equinox Meditation

Persephone awoke in Hell.
Weeping stalactites and stalagmites
extended bony fingers, trying to
touch, and smoke rose like incense
from the stony ground.

In the faint orange glow of a distant
flame, she saw Hades sleeping, long
and lost. She walked to him, and
kneeling beside him, ran her thumb
over a jagged scar on his chin, knowing

that wherever he was, Hell was not.
She knew too that without him, Heaven
was just Hell with pretty trees. And
no pomegranates. She coiled her
body around his like a snake,

listening to the breeze of his breath,
praying that spring would never come.

INCARNATION

A son of God came sporting a poncho, toting a beat up guitar.
Nobody but a few nobodies saw him for what he was
when he lit up like that and raised a dead girl with the touch
of his hand. And this dead girl, now living, she loved him,
and knelt, knowing her faith was blasphemy but heaven would be
hell without him anyway. She knelt and said I am love's humble servant,

and maybe that was the way Magdalene felt when she knelt
before that first Jesus, the one all the priests said was crazy,
that guy with dirty feet and five o'clock shadow.
Did she worry her nights away wondering if she was
worshipping an idol, or if everything her electrified skin
said was true, and she had seen the face of god?

At Noon, As Dark as Night

The photo is you standing,
sweating and startled, set against
a graying sky, your eyes mirroring the ominous clouds. Agony
skitters over your face like
a thousand invisible ants,
the African kind that eat half-dead things alive.
Behind you a church grows from grassy ground.
The needle steeple stabs high, and I think I might cry. Looking
at the cross poised on its point,
I sigh, "This boy is crucified."
They say Jesus hung for hours, howling "My god, my god,
why have you forsaken me?" Even when you smile, your eyes echo
his screams. Like a Jesus hanging perpetually above a sagging altar,
you too are frozen almost-dead, wanting something
that can only be bought with blood.

Until you, I never fantasized
holding a man child, letting him cry until his eyes grew dry and he
looked at me, the clouds there parted
like Moses's Red Sea,
like Jesus's thorn-strewn hair.

I see your eyes everywhere, and some days, when I turn
the photo on its face,
they still stare at me
as if I am a neon sign reading,
JESUS SAVES. Always,
your eyes pray
to me
begging for salvation.

1. He says this thing about throwing pearls before swine, about how it's a waste of time. I guess that's what I'm doing now, but anyway, I'll tell you how it went down, try to make you understand what's what.

The first time I saw Him was at this park one night. The air smelled like caramel corn, and little kids were hula hooping in the grass, shaking their hips and saying, "Nah, nah, nah." The festival fliers said something about entertainment, but me and my sister, we were there for the fireworks and the free food. We were walking along, chewing on cotton candy, when Missy pointed and said, "Hey, there's a guitarist."

"Holy shit," I said under my breath.

"What?" Missy asked. She had pink cotton on her lip.

I wanted to say, "That's the most beautiful thing I've ever seen," but it didn't seem right to say, so instead I asked, "Do we know Him?"

"Anne Marie! You think I'm gonna let you get all slutty with some rock star? Let's go."

I left not even knowing His name.

2. I'm not a whore. Let's get that straight.

It was weird after that, because there I was, a good little wife who couldn't stop thinking about some rock star. He had a stranglehold on my soul. When I dreamed, I'd see those burning eyes. I'd wake up sweaty between my thighs, wondering how He got that glow around Him. Like, could it have just been the stage lights? But I knew it wasn't. It was something else.

So I bided my time, did what a wife does. I cooked and cleaned. Walked around smelling like bleach and paprika. That didn't seem to bother John. Every night, he undressed right down to his socks. I don't know why, but he left those on. He mowed the lawn every Saturday, and he bought me pretty things sometimes. Flowers and earrings and once a clock shaped like a chicken. On the downside, he liked to punch holes in things. Windows. Walls. Probably would have hit me too if I didn't have the good sense to hide in the closet while he was going nuts.

But one day, I'm washing dishes, and watching the water spill from the faucet, and all of a sudden I want to suck it all down. This thirst isn't going anywhere, no matter how much I drink. And I know it's Him. So I fall to my knees and say, "Hey, Big Cheese, if you're up there, *bring* Him back to me." It's like I had Him in the first place, in some life before this one. Like He's always been mine.

Well, the next day, I go visit Missy, and she has the newspaper spread open on the bed. When I get bored and pick it up, the picture is Him. I only saw His face once before, but I could never mistake those fiery eyes. It says where He's going to be, too. He's playing a gig at some holy-roller party. They're raising funds for orphans.

"You okay?" Missy asks, pressing her hand against my forehead. Her curlers make her head look bumpy.

"Yeah," I say. "Just dizzy is all."

"You don't have a fever," she tells me.

She's wrong. This crazy's a fire that won't go away. When my sister isn't looking, I tear His picture out of the paper and fold it up in my pocket. I get back home, and all day, I keep taking it out, looking at it, mulling it over like a secret.

John comes home, sees me sitting there in his big overstuffed chair, and asks, "What're you doing in my chair, and what're you looking at anyway?"

I say, "Just some shoes I was thinking of buying."

3. When I washed His feet with my hair, it's because I felt a love that fools like you will never understand.

The place where He's singing is this little white church with a sharp steeple poking out the eye of the sky. When I tap-tap up the walkway in my high heels, the woman selling tickets looks at me funny from under her glasses, like maybe she found a roach under the couch. She doesn't like my cleavage, I guess, but I don't care, because I can hear His voice. Even from far away, it sounds like cool milk.

I go inside. There he is, all dressed in a loose shirt and tight jeans. Seeing Him does that thing it did to me the first time. I can hardly breathe. And when I shove up to the front of the stage, His eyes go wide, the way a man's eyes do when He sees you and falls in love right away. He stops playing.

You holy-rollers sitting in your pews, you don't like that. "He was just about to sing 'Amazing Grace,'" you say. Like I'm getting in the way. What *you* don't understand is that amazing grace is happening right in front of your eyes, only you're too blind to see. I don't care, because He doesn't seem to mind my coming. Just smiles a little, like He's been expecting me.

"Thank you," He whispers. My skin starts to tingle all over, like something warm is washing it, and I realize the thing on my skin is love. Love is swallowing me whole. I want to tell Him, but the words won't come. I feel this burning in my belly, and the room starts to get fuzzy. I look down, and blood is pouring out from two holes in His feet. I know it's a vision. I know it's not real. But I also know what it means. I know you fuckers are going to drill Him with holes, kill him for being something bigger than you.

I start to cry. Falling to my knees, I touch the places that show the blood, and then I start to kiss them, like the way you'd kiss a little kid if he fell down and cut himself. Just like that.

4. He has electricity in His hands. So when all of you fools look at me like I just took a dump in the corner, it doesn't matter, because He touched me.

I buy a beat-up truck and follow Him from town to town. I get to every show early and stand right there in front of His mic stand, wearing red. No matter how many shows I see, when He takes the stage, the wind gets knocked out of me. He's that beautiful. He spreads

His arms out wide and sings, not just with his mouth, but with His blood. The whole room grows quiet, like for a minute, they all know what I know. In their hearts, something tells them He's different.

I tell you, I've had that other kind of love, the one you holy-rollers talk about. My love beats your love hands down. I drive with the windows down and eat crackers and sleep in the bed of the truck, under those haloed stars, talking to the Big Cheese, having visions, knowing things. Just going where He goes, you know? The holy-rollers hate me. Sit around on their web pages and say, "Little slut, all sassy and dancing with her arms up in front of His microphone. Man, we can't even see His face through her hands. We should chop that Jezebel to pieces and feed her to the dogs. Who does she think she is?"

5. Well, it's a good question, isn't it? Who do I think I am? I'll tell you, though you don't deserve an answer. I am a girl that loves.

Love isn't something you choose. Real love is Big Cheese's best gift, and he doesn't give it lightly. You don't get to pick from a list of eligible bachelors and say, this one has nice eyes, or this one smiles right. No, love melts the eligible bachelors. Real love is a fire. Don't try to put it out. Love only burns brighter when you shove it under water. Give into it, no matter how hot it burns, how crazy it seems. Love will burn away the lies and make you into the thing you always were deep down. Love will make you a god.

6. Smug and fat and bug-eyed, you hide behind your computer screens, typing ugly things, saying, "He thinks He's better than us." I have news for you fools. He is. Him standing next to you is like a hawk standing next to a chicken—a soup hen that lives under the house and has half its feathers pulled out, all gangly and showing pink, puckered skin. You peck and you shit and you lie, and when he says you have planks in your eyes, you get pissed, and start talking about execution.

Know this. If you come for Him, in some garden, or bar room, or beach, or anywhere, you'll have to get through me, the girl in red kneeling at His feet.

"Ain't no thing," you say. "We'll do that today, slit your throat too, if we have to." Oh, I know how you holy-rollers roll. You don't have respect for anything. "All's fair in love and war," you say, but you don't know shit about love, and you make the whole world a war. He wants to make this world a better place. He says He wants to bring Heaven to Earth, and maybe you should believe Him.

So I guess this is how it'll go down. He'll be sitting on some bench in a park somewhere, and I'll see you in the bushes over there, and you'll pull out your revolver. I'll scream His name into the haloed night. Kneeling in front of Him one last time, I'll take your bullet through my spine, through the tattoo that says his name. And you might call it selfless or crazy or both when you watch my blood pooling there in the grass.

It's none of those things, and it's all those things. It's love.

21

Or what if it goes another way? What if someday you come for Him, drag Him down to the electric chair? I scream and scratch and whip my hair in your faces, but it doesn't do any good. You laugh at me. Grab my breasts. A fist to my cheek knocks me flat. My head spins while you beat Him. All I can do is say, "No, no, no."

So you fry Him. He dies. However, right before His light goes out, He looks at me, and His eyes. Man, those eyes, there's fire there, I swear. He passes it on to me. It lights up my face and hands, and in a few days' time, when He stands up at His own funeral, I'll be the one to say it first.

"It's Him. My soul's husband. He's back from the dead."

MAGDALENE'S CHRYSALIS

I learned sex from a god-man who never
touched me with his hands,
but came to me in my dreams,
made my body do things
I didn't know it could.

I married my soul's husband
in the space between night and day
rocked in his gentle arms,
swimming in the sea of colors
that separated gray reality
from the shining world behind my eyelids.

My teacher baptized me,
forgave my sins.
He bared his secret skin,
the invisible fish hieroglyph
tattooed over his sacred heart.
Smiling, my shaman taught me
the art of walking through walls.
"Look," he called, "stars come like dogs
if you call them by name."

My master impregnated me.
The seeds of his dreams grew in my belly
filled me with visions songs poems books.
In the waking world
we were prisoners.
Our love forced us to do impossible things,
grow wings to fly
through windows too high
for mortals to ever reach.

In the daytime, as we passed,

his eyes found mine,
screamed a thousand sentences
in a glance. Sometimes,
he'd catch my hand
and whisper words left over
from the midnight trances
we shared.

Our captors bared their snaggleteeth
when they saw us smiling,
but we only sang our gratitude.
"Thank you, lightless ones,
for fanning our love into a fire hot enough
to burn away our mortality
and turn us into gods."

I grow old in this prison
seemingly alone.
Anything but a crone,
when I leave my cell
the mortals want me now
more than ever.
I never tell my secret,
the reason why
my eyes have never
lost their sacred light.

I am a child of wonder.
I believe in miracles.
I have lived the magic of the chrysalis.
Brute captors, know this.
You did not win.

Amor vincit omnia.
Each night, my god moves in me.
My beloved's dreams have become my home.

An Almost Love Letter to Judas from the Crucified Magdalene

You were not The One,
could not be The One,
but still, I loved you in my way
for giving me what he would not.

He walked on water

but you walked on dirt
and let your flesh love mine
while he swore longing glances were enough
and gave everything to everyone
but the one who gave everything for him,
left me bleeding in my bed
saying I should be grateful
he even looked at me,
taunting the angels that sang my songs,
telling me I knew nothing
when really
the secrets of the universe

were scribbled on my cells.

That is how I knew what he was
what you were
what I was.
My angels whispered
I was the one
destined to fall at his feet
and kiss them.

The stories got it wrong, Judas.

When the Pharisees mocked me,
he laughed with them.
When they stoned me,
he picked up a rock.
But you, sweet Judas,
came to me and staunched
my wounds with kisses,
put a tourniquet
on the bloodied stump of my heart.

Judas, he has torn me down,

worn me down to nothing,
and you stand waiting to love me
wanting to give me everything
not understanding
that powers higher
than us all
have ordered me to love him
though he slays me.

I do.
Even now,
as I gasp my last breath,
my blood is composed of love for him.

I die every day on his cross
waiting for him to see the light
and never go blind again.
Oh, Judas,
we both got bad raps,
you a betrayer,
me a whore,
when really you were the one
who held the goddess when she cried

who kept her holy heart from evaporating
into a mist of pain.

Judas, when you met me,
my Mother gave you eyes to see I was not human.
Your beautiful lips asked me, "What are you?"
I will tell you now.
I am the sacred queen
who sheds her blood
that the god might be reborn.

I am Isis, the crucified one.

I hang here now, convulsing,
impaled by the nails
he has driven into me,
and still, he does not see me.

But you do.

And Judas,
though I cannot love you the way I love him
I wish I could run to you
as you walk away
hating me now
not seeing my cross.
If I could, I would come down
to kiss you one last time.

Judas, though mortal eyes could not see
the demons that plagued my mind
fighting to slay me
because only they and God knew what I was,
though you did not know that the light
that flowed from his bones

kept me sane
even when his flesh was cruel to me,
Judas, I did love you as much I was allowed,
and the first time you took me
saved me
made me into something other
than the disposable whore
he saw when he looked at me.
You made me less of a loveless thing.
In your arms,
I forgot the nails.

Judas, know this:
You and the angels rocked me when I wailed.
The Savior left me for dead.

Judas, you alone
knew when you met me
that I was not of this world.

Judas, gentle Judas,
you were the only one who could make me betray him
the way I did when I let you hold me.

Judas, sacred Judas,
your love for the goddess has made you holy.
You will not die a traitor's death.

Judas, beloved Judas,
If I were mortal,

I would choose you.

EUCHARIST

You stand above me, singing,
and your sweat on my neck is
baptism.

Your blood swims in my veins.
Your marrow melts with mine.
Our hands clasp, and in the invisible
gap between them, we grasp eternity.
A kiss could never be deeper than this.

Still, I want one. Every night, I dream
your lips on mine, tasting like wine and Jesus.
Your belly flat like Biblical unleavened bread,
I rest my head upon it, knowing holy. Your naval spirals
into forever. That dent in your throat renders remote

pain and possibility.
There is only now.
There is only you.
There is only me.
We three, God and us,

tangled like fish
in a net in of
stars.

Magdalene Retreats to the Cave

Climbing toward the lip of that cliff,
I recall
how I have followed my love
over the pockmarked surface of this earth,
kissing his feet,
being felled by stones thrown by madmen
who call my sight insanity.

Far more than a whore, my mind has known
mysteries reserved until now for dead things.
My skin has grown miles beyond my shell,
so that it touches All at all times.
I hide my sight, pretending to see only
three inches in front of me.

Hungry men, leave.
You will never see anything
but flesh when you look at me.
It is easier to huddle here alone
with the winged ones than to scramble
sighted
through the mud with blind things.
With no brush, how can I paint
a rainbow
for the sightless?

As moonlight wrinkles the skin of the sky
I bring my sacred bones to rest upon jagged stones.
I sing my secrets to the stars.
They whisper back.
I lay me down now in this rocky crag,
surrender myself to the breast of the earth.

My love has left me for heaven.
I am alone.
The only solace I have ever known
wraps around me like a cloud.

FROM PERSEPHONE TO HADES ON THE DAY OF HER RESURRECTION
(A SPRING EQUINOX MEDITATION)

My king,
I've slept in hell with you
for centuries
thinking if I stayed
curled around your body
like a shield
the butterflies
in my hair
would whisper to you
making you long
for spring's winged things

flight
light

I thought the stars
in my eyes
would swirl
into constellations
omens you might read
maps out of the underworld.

Light
years
later

I hear
my Mother calling for me
saying it is time for spring,
but you still storm through these
sin-singed halls
craving pomegranate seeds
and gold
barely seeing me.

Hades

Hades
Hades

how I love that scar on your chin
the dent in your throat
the way your voice quavers
when you forget to lie,
but I want none of your greed.
Your pomegranate seed
made me sick
to death
until the light in my eyes
faded, became
hell's flames.

Centuries
centuries
centuries

and still, my Mother calls to me

Persephone
Persephone
Persephone

and I miss her.
I want wings.

wind
sea

Perhaps you must see

hell
hell
hell

with no hint of heaven
to understand

exactly what
a god gives
when he sells his soul
trades love and freedom
for seeds of greed
so, beloved one,
tonight, I rode the stars
in my eyes
to my Mother.

Precious
broken
one,

I knew
you would miss me
so I tore from my belly
the seeds I ate in hell
one at a time,
never mind the pain,
scattering them over
the war torn terrain
as I flew
through Death's
open mouth,
paying Charon
the last of the seeds
for a ride across
the River Styx

a
ferry

The price for keeping
my soul was

everything
everything

I'm free. Follow me. My trail
of seeds glows behind me.

one
two
three

Hades, do not touch them. You cannot leave hell
holding her prizes in your belly.

four
five
six

The streets of hell
are paved with gold.

seven
for the
ferry

To be reborn a god
and not a death king

Hades,
marry

and enter into
my Mother's sacred spring

hungry,
humble
naked.

PART TWO

GESTATION

FISH WHISPERER

When I was a girl
I stood motionless
in still pools
cupped my hands
called fish to me.
I was never the child who wanted
thrashing things on my hook.
I simply wanted to touch them,
hold them, for a second or two.
They knew.

They came, and
I kept them
just long enough
to stroke their slick, silver scales.
After, I let them swim away
loving the currents they left
the trails of shimmer
dancing behind them
in red September sun.

You are like that,
the silverest fish I never knew.
I wanted to hold you longer,
but you slid from my hands
and swam, leaving splendid
tsunamis in your wake.

I wonder if I will drown.

GESTATION

My mother's heartbeat
sings to me. Here,
wrapped red in
the spongy cradle
of her womb,
I touch God with
my intestines. I can hear
Her inside me whispering.
"This One is Mine," she says.
Liquid light drips down
the buttons of my back.

MORDEDURA DE SERPIENTE

Today, my blood is composed primarily of white wine. I drank it last night in lieu of red to keep you from mistaking me for a thing with gory teeth, a vampy wolverine. You played your guitar, and I watched the strings, thinking things no nice girl should ever think about fingers. *Señoritas* danced around you, *mariposa* tattoos fluttering. In my head, I said, "I want to be your butterfly specimen, brittle on your board, brilliant wings pinned."

At the *mercado*, the woman said, "Almost free for you," as you sorted through silver things. You picked out a cobra ring, and I wondered who the snake was, me or you. In my head, I said, "I want you to bite me on the neck. I want to die screaming with your venom in my veins."

As I slid the ring on your finger, you smiled. Your calluses were like braille. Time slowed, and dust mites glowed like embers from an ancient fire. *"Quanto es?"* When you spoke, you were a bomb, exploding the world around you. Inside my head, I said, "I want to crawl inside your fire, let you burn me down to bones."

Shelved sugar skulls watched, leering. *"La suerte está echada,"* they whispered. Were it not for the ceramic saints shushing me, I might have said vile things about that ring, fallen to my knees, wrapped my tongue around your finger like the silver snake, swallowed it whole.

SACRAMENT

The Mexican rain rides bolts of blue lightning
dismounting on the hot, cracked ground that is so
like the sound of your voice. I am here,

in the land of Diego Rivera and Frida Kahlo
riding bolts of this love, so thick it can only
be rendered in paint or blood. She said

"painters paint, weavers weave, and Frida
Diegos," making him into The Verb. For me,
you are The Verb, my reason to breathe. Today,

in the *jardin*, when the swelling sun and the scent
of gardenias left me dizzy, the only thing I could think
was, I wish I could give this moment to you, wrap it up

in corn husks like a tamale and deliver
it to you on a silver plate. Here,
churches swallow saint's bones.

They tuck skulls away in their dark mouths, in the walls,
in the floors. Mary Magdalene's pitted tibia soaks up
the colors of the stained glass glinting in the setting sun.

My bones are buried in the church of you.

Human Sacrifice

Sell me a fantasy, Momma.
Tell about white horses and knights who use their swords
to slay dragons but never to slit your throat. Tell about self-cleaning
castles in the clouds where cobwebs only live in dank
dungeons, places you never go, so who needs a feather duster?
Tell about maidens who do not stain blood red when they sin.

Sell me a fantasy, Momma.
Tell about happily-ever-after with no bruises. Tell about
thrusting your silky hands into beehives and coming out
with fistfuls of honey without getting stung even once.
And you can eat butter all day and night, and never
an ounce of cellulite mars your princess thighs.

Sell me a fantasy momma
Tell about living forever, or when you finally do die
it is of old age, but you are still young. Your face is milky.
Your breasts never droop. You lie in a glass casket with roses
entwined in your hair, smiling slightly because you know
your prince will never use Excalibur to slaughter your children.

Sell me a fantasy momma. I have a nickel
and three pennies,
and it is getting dark,
and I am beginning to believe
more in the witches that live under my bed
than I ever once believed in forever.

Sell me a fantasy, Momma.
I will trade my milky skin,
the rose-tipped crests that are my breasts,
the bloodied rosebud that smolders between my thighs
for a chance to hold your cloud-shrouded castle
in the palm of my hand just once.

From Davida To Goliath

My darling, I am not afraid of you
as you stand, spear in hand
brandishing hate and flashing armor.
Say what you will.
I stand on the land that belongs
to my mother.
This river is the water that flowed from her womb
as I slipped into this world.

WITCH'S CURSE

There is an eye
behind my eyes
where secrets come to me
unbidden
hidden things
I would rather not know.
I ask them to leave me,
but it seems
the chosen of the gods
can never be
unchosen.

Would I live as a mortal
if I could?
What would I give to sit with them
in the marketplace
talking, laughing,
eating yeasty bread
not knowing the secrets sands
shifting in the deserts of their heads.
Oh, to be blind
to simply believe
that grass was only grass
that stars were only stars
to not have a mind that leapt
to the ragged corners of eternity
questioning angels.

If only the angels didn't answer.

I have seen
God.
You ask me to unsee Her now

calling my lucidity
insanity,
and how can I explain
what I know?
How can I tell you that I have watched
dead things rise again,
that I do not have the luxury
of doubt?
You will never see the things I do.

I could tell you what is coming
strumming strings
on the guitar of the future
until they speak
pouring out prophecies,
but you would not believe me.
You would call it coincidence.
Or worse, you would call me a devil
strip me naked
flay me in the streets
offer my meat on a pyre
to the vile thing

you call God.

Our flesh is the same,
but our souls came
from different worlds.
This is my curse.
I must pretend
every second of every day
to be one of you.
This life, I know how to behave
hiding my light under a bushel.

Men have loved me, but

one by one,
they saw the sun in my eyes
called it Satan,
stumbled onto my magic
(sometimes it slips out unbidden)
and sentenced me:

possessed.

The Christ whose name you have profaned,
my only husband,
whispers in my ear each night,
comforts me
calling me "beloved."

Be glad that my path
is paved with love. Were I to take off my gloves,
my Mother's light might flow from my fingers,
incinerate you where you stand.
This is no fairy tale, no child's game.
The power that lives in my hands
scares even me. Try as I might
I cannot begrudge you your fear.

The Goddess in me Unkneels

I have basked in the blue light of ghosts
sunbathed in the glow of hell's flames
given chunks of my best meat
to the devil's dogs, for what?
Pearl's before swine, he said.

I push pearls from the oyster of my womb's eye
and toss them under the hooved feet of ghosts
waiting for their iron tusks to turn, tear me to pieces.
Kneeling, I ask, "For what
do I give these dogs my best meat?"

I do not want my story to end here, with my best meat
given to the dogs, with my clouded eyes
watching my pearls disappear under hooves, for what,
into the blue flecked slime of ghosts?
I will stand, reach into the flames
to take the hand of the goddess who it is said

looms a head taller than all who say
I should kneel, those dogs who ate my best meat.
I will take her hand here in the flames
and together we will gather our pearls, our eyes.
I will bury them in her mouth, hide from the ghosts
those pearls I have tossed before swine. For what?

And she will swallow my pearls, and wait for what
will gestate. She said
in her belly the pearls will become seeds, more than meat
for dogs. I will lend the blue light back to the ghosts.
I will gather the sky's blue into my eyes,
my strength into my hand as it floats unsinged in the flames

She stands in the flames.
The goddess is me. Waiting for what
will gestate. Her eyes
are the blue white of pearls. It is said
they shine with the light of ghosts.
Her arms are spread wide ready to meet

this child, born of ghost light and flame
whose meat will never be given to dogs. What
I see is the child of the goddess burning behind my eyes.

Twilight Song

To me, you have been the sea,
mighty cold crashing impenetrable.
Awe-inspiring. Naked, I dove in
and drowned again and again and again.

And yet, now, worn thin, shivering here
on the jagged cliff overlooking your shore, I
see a thing that you never were to me. A
stream. I don't want to drown anymore.

I want to paint you with shades I've
never opened, at twilight, when
the sun isn't shining, and your water
grows green and gray in dying day.

I want to dip my bare feet in you, bleed when your
sharp stones cut my toes. I want to watch mist rising
from your skin, to know that if I don't water you
with my sins, you might just dry up.

I want to bathe in your stagnant secrets,
the silent pools that stink. I want to be
bitten by the crabs that live under
the shards of rotting bark in your bed.

I want your leeches to slither up my legs
and suck my blood. I want to pet the fat,
cat-faced carp that dwells in your blackest
mud, gorging himself on your lies.

The god I found in you was me all along.
I don't need to drown in a god anymore.
I want to lie, dying, in the mud from which
I came, with a man, just a man, made of the same.

Unmetered Unrhymed Unsonnet Scrawled by Heaven's Child

Tonight, I am a shooting star. I stand naked, astonished
by my own beauty, by the light seeping out of the tips of my
fingers, the knobs of my knees, the buttons of my back.

Tonight, I shine like a thousand constellations rolled
into one, Pleiades and the Virgin and Saturn with her
crystalline rings thrown in for good measure.

Tonight, I dance in time to the beat
of the stars as they sing and spin
in their watery heaven.

Tonight, I touch God with my intestines. I can hear
Her in my belly whispering that there is something else
and nothing else. That I am, and I am is enough. That this,

tonight, this is heaven, here, touching Her face and singing
Her songs and dancing Her dance, My dance that ripples
down the buttons of my back into my toes.

The thing with me is this. I believed it
when my daddy told me
I was Heaven's Child.

Theology

All the angels I know are alcoholics.
They can't stand the sight of blood, so they drink it away.
All the devils I know donate to charity.
Publicly.
They leave big tips when people are watching.
Most demons can quote The Bible in a pinch,
when it serves them.

All of the gods I know wander through life blinking,
befuddled,
accidentally leaving miracles in their wake.
All of the goddesses I know have a penchant for cheeses and pastries.
They trip often, enchanted as they are by the round edges of clouds.
Most mortals write divine ones off as lunatics,
keep their worlds safe and sane.

I have read holy scriptures in the lined faces of old women
begging for bread.

I have heard the Creator whisper secrets in the quiet places trapped
between the notes of rock-n-roll songs.

The only book you ever needed was written on your heart before you born.

The only God that counts dances inside of you, moved by the
pounding of your blood.

A Message to the Mad Ones

You say it is impossible to do the things we do,
walk on water, drift through walls like mist.
Impossible for you, maybe.
When we show you the magic that lives in our bones,
you call us mad,
wrapping us in the loveless arms of straightjackets.

Poisoning our sacred blood with pills,
you silence the voices of the unseen ones
that would lead us to freedom.
You suffocate our ironclad wills
under mountains of
propaganda.
Sit down, shut up, step in line, you say
strangling the fiery, singing thing in our bellies
that was born to disobey.
Given to cowardice,
you kill all that your
tiny minds
cannot comprehend.
With fire and sword,
you purge us of our innocence
calling the lightning that flashes in our eyes
Satan.
God in heaven hates witches, you scream. *You will burn for eternity if you
dare to seize your now.* With your blasphemous religion, you cut off our
conversation
with the God that
spins in the very molecules of the holy air
we breathe.
What must we pay
for your worthless label
of sanity?

How much of our flesh
must we carve away
before you deign to acknowledge our ethereal beauty?
Our very lives
the minutes the hours the days
that make up our existence
must be sacrificed on your altar,
our holy bodies atrophying in cubicles,
our brilliant minds withering,
crunching numbers endlessly.
Your lies have consigned us to futility.
Hypnotized, we stare at your screens,
pressing buttons like lab rats,
hungry for one more "like."
Your sanity, dead ones,
is insanity,
a life cut off from all that is
striving for the airbrushed lie
you say should be,
a hopeless existence that prizes imaginary symbols
over tangible things,
invisible numbers in invisible bank accounts
over flesh and blood, breathing beings.
You live in the future
and the past
places that don't exist
in reality.
And you call us crazy?
We are born whole,
but you convince us we are half of something,
bribing us with diamonds, dresses, and tiered confections,
injecting us with the infection of your fantasy,
consigning us to lives of lonely resignation,
marrying us to monsters,
calling this bondage love.

When the sacred dove visits,
we run
terrified of sinning
against an institution
based on the illusion of possession
of that which can never be possessed.
We are the next step in evolution.
Our DNA has granted us powers
you can't comprehend.
You were born sightless
in a world of wonders,
so you gouge out the eyes
of the sighted ones
and brand their vision
lunacy.
Our miracles are not supernatural.
Five-hundred years ago
electricity would have been revered as sorcery.
So are we
science that has yet to be explained.
All is natural. All is magic.
You cannot understand what we see
anymore than an ant can understand
you.
Never mind, blind things.
We will rise on winds breathed by gods you deem long dead,
riding wings made from iridescent feathers you can't see.
Our wise souls
will heal every cell in the body
of this convulsing, precious planet.
Quake not, trembling ones.
Ours is not an apocalypse of fire
but an ecstatic lifting
a ripping of the veil of illusion
to reveal the heaven

that is buried here even now.
There is no such thing as damnation.
You too will be saved.
Beloved, broken things, know this.
Underneath the lies you have believed, you are already perfect.
The nightmare is already ending.
When the top-40-hits and laugh tracks and freeways grow silent,
voices you are not yet equipped to hear
sing endlessly of dawn.

WE ARE WOMEN

We are women.

We have come to this not
through rash of fuzz on chin or quavering of voice
but through blood.
Our strength is in our work-worn hands,
our milk swollen breasts, our heavy thighs
in the gentle swell of our bellies and the callus on our heels.
Our strength is in the pear of our womb.
We do not wield spear or machete or rifle.
We need not show our power by the taking of life.
We are the lifegivers.
In times of harvest
we groan among fallen sheaves of wheat
drowning in dying sunlight.
We push from our bodies the souls of women and men.
In the flickering night
we wipe the blood from our thighs
rise on tremulous legs
having lashed to our breast the one
we loved enough to die and rise again for
having given our milk and our blood and our water and our tears
so that another may live.

And you, time.

You have called us weak.
You have painted us again and again and again
in black and white
frail and soft and timid
but never strong.
You have robbed from us the colors that pulse in
our bodies and our smiles and the creases of our eyes.

You have wrapped a chain around our thighs
and a gall soaked rag around our lips.
And you have called this love.
You have stolen from us our passion,
ignoring the thrusting of our hips
the swelling of our breasts
the ripeness of our thighs.
You have smothered between your hardened hands
our minds
suffocating ancient wisdoms
books, poems, theorems, dreams.
You have given us a gravelly place under the feet of men,
leaving us to be trampled again and again and again
by boots made for fighting.

Yet we have survived.

And you have called us weak.
We have survived
rules of thumb, witch hunts, rapes.
We have carried in our bosoms the flame of life
the strength to walk on when legs scream lie down
the wisdom to speak when lips cry shut up.
We have thrashed on through the ocean of life
with leviathans looming all around
with seaweed wrapped around our eyes
with mouths full of bitter water
we have struggled on.
And now, time.

Now, we gather.

The women.
We gather our breasts and our minds
and our hands and our legs and our mouths.

We burn the chains that have bound us
and spit from between our lips the gall soaked rag
we have chewed on for so long.
We will not keep silent.
We will break out the vibrant watercolors
and paint ourselves as we truly are
naked and wild and free and strong.
Unbroken.
We will take your rules
and your witch hunts
and your rapes
and shove them down your throat.
We will rise above the feet of men.
We will call to ourselves dolphins and whales
and ride them through mother earth's oceans

laughing and singing.
We will dance upon their silken skin and call them sisters.
We are women.

We are not lilacs or daisies or gardenias.
We are yuccas.
Strong and sharp
our flowers bright like the sun
able to live on in the desert
able to survive without water.

We are women.

Our silence has come to an end.

PART THREE

FROM ISIS TO OSIRIS

Book of the Dead

I close my eyes,
and Osiris's ladder descends
from heavens
torn by unseen hands.
Stars shake loose
fill my eyes
with the red cries of the

dying

that fled to them
as they bled,
found solace
in radiant

forever.

Oh, clever Set
how you lied
when you said
the dead
would be judged
by a sharp toothed dragon.
When I look into the eyes
of this death god,
He is love incarnate.

Resurrection.

His gaze holds thick secrets
that cannot be spoken
by mortal tongues.
Light more blinding than sun.

A spiral stretching on and on and on
into the dark matter of

eternity.

There is no fear here,
only the silent solace of knowing
I am finally
going

home.

FROM ISIS TO SET WHEN OSIRIS LAY DREAMING IN HIS COFFIN

Scene: Isis loves Osiris. Twin light-beings, they rule Egypt with grace and dignity. Egypt flourishes, becomes a paradise. The vile god of chaos, Set, gets jealous, wants Osiris's crown. He tricks, traps, and kills Osiris, turning Egypt into hell. His minions cavort in the once sacred temple, filling it with deception, debauchery, and death. If not for Isis's love, the story might end there, in apocalyptic tragedy. But Isis cannot give up on her sacred other half.

Ugly one,
I will be the sand in your panties
the mare in your nights
the sight that makes
your reptile blood
run hot.
Ever present,
I will be the thing
that reminds you
the vile ring
you have placed on his finger
is fool's gold.

Cowering one,
you and I are not
fashioned from the same stuff
so you do not understand
the way I flinch-less sing
in the face of cannon fire.
My spine is forged of steel.
I will stand and stand and stand
until your foul gates crumble,
my love crawls from the rubble,
and his sacred hand slides into mine.

Petty, pretty-less one,
greed is no match for love.
Lie and lie and lie.
Make him die and die and die,
but know
that every time
his lights go out
he dreams himself in my bed.

Shrieking one,
I will stop kicking your head
let you slither away with your un-dead daddy
the day you give me back
my husband.
When all is said and done,
I will be the one
who writes our story.
You will go down in the
Book of the Dead
as the jealous joke
that tried to usurp a throne
and found herself
in a single-wide alone
with her entourage of bloated crones
sipping Pabst Blue Ribbon.

(Defeated one,
don't despair.
I hear those new trailers
have refrigerated air
and deluxe pressed wood paneling.)

Isis Demands a Stand

Osiris, see this black?
I mourn today, sick to death of seeing your light
hijacked by slack-jawed lackies. Pagan gods dance
around you, chanting their Satanic creed.
Scheming and screaming, they have chained you
to their loveless greed, whored you out
to a graceless, mortal thing. Impostors,
pretenders to your empty throne
(they can't climb into it even though they try),
they see me, and never see me at all.
Sneering, they ogle my ass and thighs
ignoring the lightning in my eyes.
I let them. Sleight of hand, or sleight of breast.
See my body. Don't see the rest. Fools
too dumb to know I've come to rescue you.
Only the holy know the holy when they meet it.

(Dear zombies, clumsy, artless things,
lust for these lips, blind to the fluttering of
my falcon wings. I bide my time, watching you
watch Him. You think He is a thing.
When He smiles, all you see is teeth.
The sacred light in His eyes flashed.
You shrieked, "Let's bottle it! Make some cash!"
How dare you try to own His might?
Do you not know He is the rising sun,
The One born to bring the dawn?
My Holy Mother Nut is inconsolable,
weeping for her stolen son.)

Osiris, stand up. Fight.

You have more might in your tiny toe

than they have in all of their doughy flesh.
When you rise, the universe will conspire
to bring you all that you desire and more.
But first you must let me save you. Heaven
rewards the brave. Take my hand.
I sold seven strands of my fiery hair to buy
two one-way tickets to The Promised Land.
Climb out of the gold-plated grave they dug for you.

My love, let me love you.
Your splendid flesh was never meant
to be a mausoleum for blanched bones.

From Isis to Osiris on the Day She Found His Head

Beloved,
what you do not know
what you will never know
what you cannot know
because you are dead
is the day that monster
severed your head
my throat was cut.

Beloved,
my blood flooded the Nile
until it swelled red
overflowing its banks
deluging the land in gore.
Crocodiles roared in anguish.
Bastet cast aside her cobra crown.
I waded into the wicked waters
praying I would drown.

Beloved,
the jackal bitch who took your head
smirked as she gutted you,
but the worst thing
was the way she
slipped your signet ring
on her vile finger
and filled your skull
with her secret sins
until your fiery eyes grew
flat and dead like tar.

Beloved,
The Nile may weep blood

for a thousand years
but crimson tears cannot wash clean
the grief I knew when I saw
my shorn husband's head
held aloft by a demon whore.

Scribe Ani,
write this truth
in your Book of the Dead:
When I found Osiris's hands
buried in the bloody mud,
It was I who became
an amputee.

What Isis Sang as She Passed Him Through the Fire

Ever devoted to resurrecting her husband, Isis goes to the house where his body is now sequestered and presents herself as a nursemaid for the queen's son. Isis falls in love with the child and decides to gift him with divinity. To make him a god, she must pass him through an eternal fire. She sings as she does so, casting a loving spell to make the boy an immortal thing.

My baby daddy was a golden phallus.
My palace is three-billion light-years high,
hewn from the bones of the first bonsai tree,
lighted by the gleaming eye
I tore from Satan's skull
the day I stole his head.
My towers reach far beyond the sky
as you know it.
I am a splendid magic thing,
bride of the eternal king.
Those stars up there?
Sweat drops I wiped
from my inner thigh
so I could wear them in my hair.

I won't just make your blood pound.
I'll reverse its course. I'll reinforce
your bones with stone. My kiss
will bring you to your knees,
give you visions and dreams.

Your screams of ecstasy will echo
'round the Milky Way. Turn night to day.
I'll remix your heartbeat,
turn your breaths into heat waves,
your groans into serenades.

Though my song buckles your spine,
this love of mine will be the thing that saves you,
turns your cringing peasant into a king,
your stammering coward into a fearless, evermore thing.

I'll teach you the true religion of the catacombs.
You'll meet Osiris on his feathered throne.
Isis injection.
Kid, I'll infect you with resurrection.
You dig? Though you die, yet shall you live.

Death is a mask.
Yank it off.
Sing for your life.
Make me your eternal wife.
Even my lies are true.
Swallow my fire.
Incinerate your facade.
Your golden core will emerge unburned.

Mortal child, exit my flames a
god.

Isis Declares War

Hideous jackal prince,
betraying brother, slayer of souls,
devourer of worlds, pitiful pretender
to my husband's holy throne
know this.
I am coming for you.

I come not in my own might
for I own no might.
I come without armor.
Armor is too heavy for me
I come without an army.
My army has been swallowed,
drowned in the bowels of your roiling sea.

See this hand. It is empty
save this spot here
where Osiris touched me once.
It burns still with his warmth
has sustained me through years of wandering
will grow to become the flame that consumes you.
What I hold in my palm is my heaven
and your hell. It is that same fire
you quiver to see in his eyes.
When I slept in the leviathan's belly
I dreamed it, and it kept me alive.

I come to you not in my own name.
I come in the name of my holy mother Nut
who weeps endlessly for her stolen son.
I come in the name of my sacred father Ra
the genesis of the Rising Sun.
I come to you in the name of a love

too pure for you to understand.
I come to you in the name of the fire
in my hand, the let-there-be that created galaxies,
the gravity that holds atoms together.

You are a schemer, but what use are schemes
against visions and dreams? Can your gem-studded sabers
bring down invisible angels? You are a liar, but what good
are lies in the face of the radiant nakedness of my truth?
You own an empire, and I own only this
speck of love. Within it sleeps a universe.

ISIS CALLS FOR RESURRECTION (AKA: LOVE SONG FOR A REANI-
MATED CORPSE)

Baby, they don't call me
a love goddess for nothing.

I have fallen in love so many times
with white caps on waves
and headstones on graves
bearing images of mossy angels.
But Osiris, you slew me
the way David stoned Goliath dead.
Your might was the rightest thing I had
ever known. A sunbaked moonstone,
I burned, wanting you inside me
until I realized you already were
my bones, the throne upon which
the goddess in me rested.

Your head is shrinking down to dead
and so what? Gray haired, washed up,
they said, but your eyes still gleam
and kneeling, wailing, I wait for your doubt
to be sated, for you to be seated again
upon the throne that is yours.
Know this. My ribcage is the stage
upon which you must plant your boots
and stand.

My love, forget not
that you are a hurricane.
Even dead, you uproot villages.
And though hell pillages heaven
my pilgrimages to your grave
will not stop until at last

the earth quakes and you rise,
singing, to shake the ground
you walk on. Today,
slack-jawed lackeys
keep you chained.

Hungry crows and grackles
creep over sacred ground
but not for long.

My pendulum swings
and cherubim wing from sepulchers
ready to kiss dead lips alive.

From Isis to Set When She Banished Him to the Arizona Desert (Which is Something Like Hell but Hotter)

Darling, you fucked up tonight
rattling the leash you dared clamp
on my husband's sacred neck
mocking me, reminding me of
my place
in your two-bit, mortal scene.
Fat man, see that throne?
My mother made it for me
from the skulls of
pagan gods.
Rapists.
Murderers.
Lawless, loveless things.
The footstool bears the image of the face
of a demon who dared try
pulling rank on me.
That throne is
my place,
given to me
by the Heavenly Queen
long before you were
an itch in your demon daddy's undies.
Still, my seat might be uncomfortable
fashioned as it is from blanched bones.
It could use a cushion before I ascend.
A fat man should do nicely.

Darling, let's speak of
your place.
I declare that by this time
next year
you and your soulless spawn

will be living in a trailer
drinking moonshine
and screwtop wine
from broken bottles.
Your hell will hold no fire.
Nothing so grand as that.
A double wide in the desert
waits for you, oh fat man.
When you are banished there,
remember me. See my face,
oh, scheming Set,
in your new home's peeling linoleum,
dripping faucets,
cheap, warped paneling.
I will leave
a saguaro in your yard
something green
to lend you shade.
You are so vile
you've reduced me
a love goddess
to just that shred of mercy.

Darling,
I hope
you like
plastic
flamingos.

From Isis to Osiris on the Day She Gave Him Back His Breath

My twin, I rocked with you
in the warm current
of our mother's sacred sea.
Holding hands
we rode a wave
of her blood
onto Egypt's rocky soil.
The sun first rose, tore the night, when you opened your eyes to
shine into the light of mine. The world grew in the space between
our pressed together palms.
The prophecies said you would die, but I never knew grief
would swallow me whole
when the monster slew my brother before my eyes. Grinning,
he held up that leg
with your shoe on the end.
My magic bled into madness.
All these years, I have wandered,
my heels torn, my haunted eyes replaying again and again
the sight of your blood draining
staining white sand.
I found your hand atop a tree. Your head in red river mud. I kissed
each one as if you were in them, wore them like jewelry,
ornaments on a death tree.
My brother,
my love,
my light bringer,
my king,
this mad thing
I became was not
pretty.
When the doves sang
of my insanity

I could not disagree.
Look at me.
Shrouded in black, I add
this last finger to the stack of death that was once you.
I reassemble the puzzle.
Madness, yes.
I believe in madness.
I believe in magic.
I believe in the mess,
the miracle of you.
My brother,
my twin,
my husband,
calling on all the madness
in my sacred soul,
I press my lips
against your
dead ones
remembering your smile.
I cannot leave you cold in this lightless place.
"Mother," I whisper, "you gave him life once. Let him live again.
Without him, there is no magic,
only madness
left of me."

From the corner of my eye
I see your tiny finger move.

From Isis To Osiris When She Woke From a Wet Dream

And while all I've said about sacred love is ineffable
and true, tonight while I sprawled here sleeping, my *ka*
burned through walls to you to see if you would show
me what you do when taboo doesn't matter.

Once, you danced. Your shirt crept high, flaunting
skin I had never seen. Your sweat ran like rivers
of holy water. It sanctified the obscene.
Tonight, I dreamed you baptized me.

Damn Father Time and his clumsy hands
that crammed me into the Virgin Mary's shell.
My body burns like hell tonight, wanting things
anything but customary for a pristine heavenly queen.

I am goddess. I am all. I am sacred
and profane, and on this plane when I
come dressed in skin, it flushes
when I think of sinning with you.

I fall to my knees and worship.
The sacred cows moan moo.
Let the choir scream.
Amen.

From Isis to Osiris on the Day of His Resurrection

And so I found you sleeping in that tree. The branches cradling your body
were my arms. I called you down. When demons sing my song,
they say my voice was like thunder. Only angels understand
it was as gentle as the rain. Osiris, your name to me was love,

and you came shattered in a million pieces like a dropped vase upon
the stony ground. Watering you with my tears, I imagined your dead hands
as they had once been hot upon my throat. I remembered the way
your slack mouth used to laugh when you were bold with wine.

And so the pieces of you flew and grew together. As they opened, your eyes
blinded me with light. Even gods sometimes forget to believe, but I will

never

doubt again because I saw Genesis. I saw, "Let there be light." I saw comets
explode into being and melt together to become the sun in your eyes.

From Isis to Osiris: Song for the Resurrection of a Fallen God

My phoenix, the dawn is breaking.

Sirius rises.

Rise too from the ashes.
Leave behind the embers of the crucible
and follow me
as I soar into the night sky
a glorious egg
shattering
scattering light
to the farthest reaches of the horizon.

Darling,
leave behind the cinders
of our Calvary
and rise with me.
Do not mistake
the crucible for the fire.
Without me
it is a cold, dead thing.

Beloved, do not mistake
the crucible for me.
It burned because
I lived there long enough
to show you the way.
Grab the tail of the comet
that is me
and soar behind me
into the newborn sun.

Already, my radiant wings

span stars.

My king, do not mistake
the crucible for love.
It was in the dragon's belly
that our mortality burned away,
leaving us the gods
we were born to be.

Osiris, follow me.
The night sky awaits your rising.
You cannot fight fate.
Strong one, your might
is nothing in the face of eternity.
Destiny is calling, my king.

Rise up.

Leave behind the crucible,
the dead remnant
of my resurrection.

My shroud
smothers death.
Having shed
my mortal skin

I rise.
I rise.
I rise.

Osiris, my love,
eternal burning,
living one,
leave behind

the shards
of our chrysalis,
shatter,
scatter your light
to the four edges of the horizon.

Rise.
Rise.
Rise.

Arise, beloved, winged thing.
Fear not.
Hell could not hold me.
Death has lost its sting.
I have paved the way for life.

Amor Vincit Omnia.

Rise up,
and follow me.

ACKNOWLEDGMENTS

Dedication: For my love, The Shining One. All of the poems that matter are yours.

Acknowledgements: This book represents the collected works of a decade of my life, perhaps the most magical and adventurous decade thus far. Much of it was written on airplanes and at truck stops and in motel rooms with pentagrams carved into the walls as I followed Roger Clyne (whose very existence proves to me that God is) and his wonderful band members, Jim Dalton, Nick Scropos, and P.H. Naffah, all around the globe. I thank the Peacemakers for making my life a zillion times more beautiful than it ever would have been had I not stumbled upon them all those years ago. Although my name on the band's internet bulletin board was Siren Song, this book title was Jeni Stewart's idea, not mine. The breathtaking interior art, featuring me as a mermaid, was spontaneously created by the incredible Jason Hicks, who had no knowledge of my mermaid-esque moniker. Is the universe conspiring to make me a mermaid? Maybe. If I sprout a fish tail, I'll know for sure.

I thank my amazing children, Desi and Tim, for being my most compelling inspirations, the greatest loves of my life, and my 24/7 reasons to believe the world is a bright and benevolent place.

I am eternally grateful to the lovely, brilliant Jeni Stewart for her unfaltering belief in me and my work, for not doubting my sanity (even when I am kissing taxidermied squirrels in speakeasies), for deciding my poetry was worth publishing in book form, and for being such an indispensable part of my life, literary and otherwise. I love you, woman. But then, you know that.

I am also endlessly grateful to Jeni's counterpart, the illustrious Daniel Wallace, who single-handedly revives my faith in the male half of the human race while simultaneously making me give up on photobombing forever because no way can I match his extraordinary technique. (Jazz hands!)

I am indebted to my brilliant mentors, Joseph and Amanda Boyden, who inspired me to believe in my words, conspired with me on Mexican rooftops, and taught me everything there was to know about writing (although I'm pretty sure I still don't follow the rules very well).

To my unfailing soul sisters, Julie Barrett, Polyxeni Angelis, Martine Tharp, Merridith Allen, Tonya Thompson, and Jessica Willson, without whom I am 100% certain I would be dead. Is love a big enough word for what I feel for you? I don't think it is.

To my mother and brother, who I thank much more profusely in my novel because I'm not sure they'll want to be mentioned here, but have loved me through so much, have taught me to live with dignity and kindness, have been my rocks through so many war-torn years.

To my the best man I have ever known, my father, who gave me enough love in 21 years to sustain me for a lifetime.

To Eric Auxier, my kick-ass ex-husband and unfaltering friend, who never, ever gave up on my writing, even when I gave up on it myself. Without your support, Cap'n Aux, I'd be living in a cardboard box licking residue from soup cans. You are proof to me that love can last a lifetime, even if it changes forms.

To Jesus, who I am 100% convinced digs me, despite my irreverence, and manages to keep me alive, despite of my foibles. (Daniel says when I'm with Jeni, Jesus says, "Oh, thank God. Jeni's got her. I get a day off.")

And to Big Momma. Because really, pretty lady, what would I do without you?

Tawni Waters is a writer, actor, college teacher, and gypsy. Her first novel, *Beauty of the Broken*, was released by Simon/Pulse in Fall 2014. Her work has been published in *Best Travel Writing 2010*, *Bridal Guide Magazine*, and many other magazines and journals. She is a regular contributor to *The Burlesque Press Variety Show* where she maintains a devoted following. She teaches creative writing at Estrella Mountain College. She lives in Phoenix, Arizona with her children and a menagerie of wayward animals. In her spare time, she talks to angels, humanely evicts spiders from her floorboards, and plays Magdalene to a minor rock god.

⚜

THIS BOOK'S TYPE:

Siren Song's interior text is set in Garamond. The text on the spine is set in Bizon, by Axel Bizon.